Fluminense

ANIMALS

Honey possum

HONEY BEES

BONGO

This edition published in 2014
First published in 2013
Copyright© Marshall Editions 2013

Paca

Swallowtail butterfly

QED Publishing
A Quarto Group company
The Old Brewery,
6 Blundell Street,
London, N7 9BH
ISBN 978 1 78171 911 4

Printed in China
by 1010 Printing International Ltd

EMPEROR ANGEL FISH

Sandgrouse

TIGER

BUTTERFLY FISH

Wahoo fish

Moorish idol fish

BEE

Corroboree frog

Mellor's chameleon

ANIMALS

Camilla de la Bedoyere

Clown anemonefish

Coral snake

QED

QED Publishing

Blue-tongued skink

ZEBRA

Prairie chicken

RING TAILED LEMUR

Geometrid moth

FLYING LEMUR

TOAD

Paradise tree snake

GUPPY

Jewel beetle

Tragopan

PLAICE

Garden spider

Civet

Tiger beetle

WHALE SHARK

PEACOCK

Whalefish

Ladybird

Anaconda

Turtle

NARWHAL

Salamander

Leopard

DOLPHINFISH

Red howler monkey

RED SALAMANDER

Clown anemonefish

Red

RED FOX

Cardinal

VELVET MITE

Scarlet
tanager

Roughie

Siamese fightingfish

Shieldbug

SHRIMP

RED KANGAROO

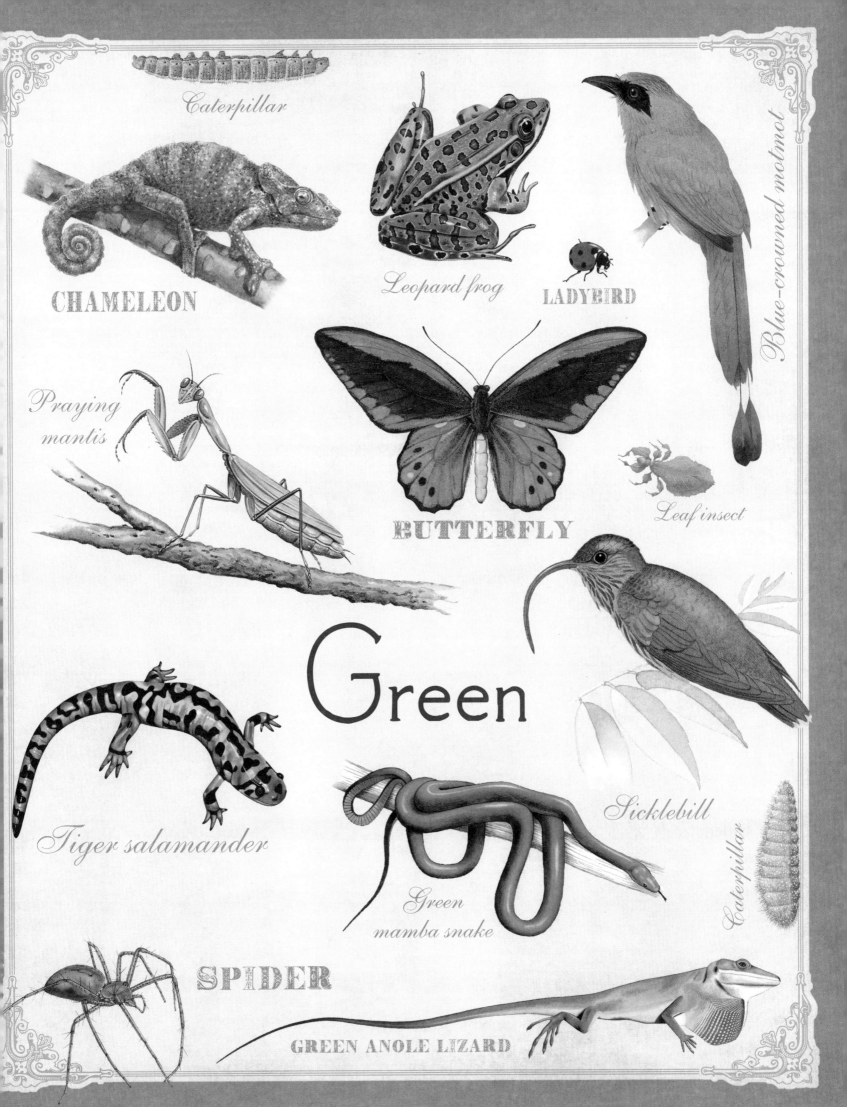

Caterpillar

CHAMELEON

Leopard frog

LADYBIRD

Blue-crowned motmot

Praying mantis

BUTTERFLY

Leaf insect

Green

Tiger salamander

Sicklebill

Caterpillar

SPIDER

Green mamba snake

GREEN ANOLE LIZARD

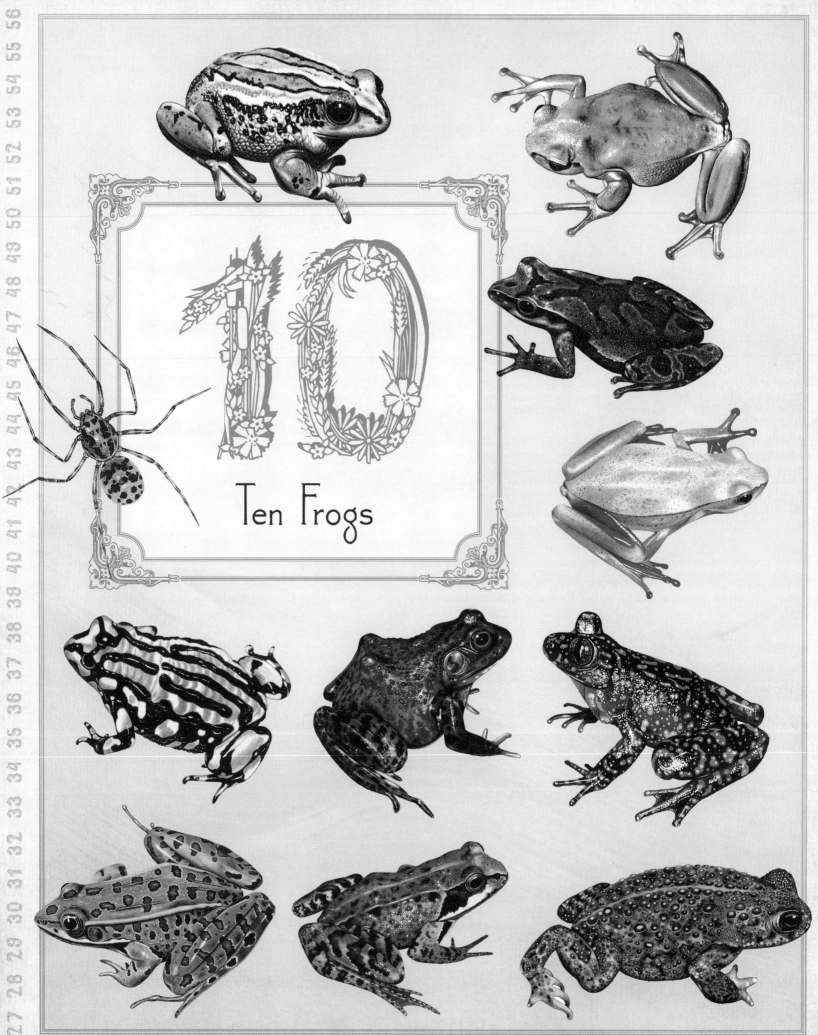

10

Ten Frogs

20

Twenty Spiders

SPECTACLED CAIMAN

Rough-head grenadier

HAMMERHEAD SHARK

Blowfly

SNOWY OWL

Wolf spider

Bee

Plaice

LOCUST

Web-footed gecko

SQUID

Most animals have two eyes – which of these creatures has more than two?

Bee

NAUTILUS

Aye-aye

Lamp shell

TURTLE

Swallowtail butterfly

ARUM LILY
FROG

Yellow

Golden oriole

YELLOWTAIL
SNAPPER

Plant bug

BLUE
TANG

*Yellow-throated
longclaw*

Crab spider

Thorny starfish

GREATER FRUIT BAT

HARVEST MOUSE

Click beetle

Golden poison-arrow frog

Orange

ORANGUTAN

Mettalmark butterfly

GOLDFISH

ATLAS MOTH

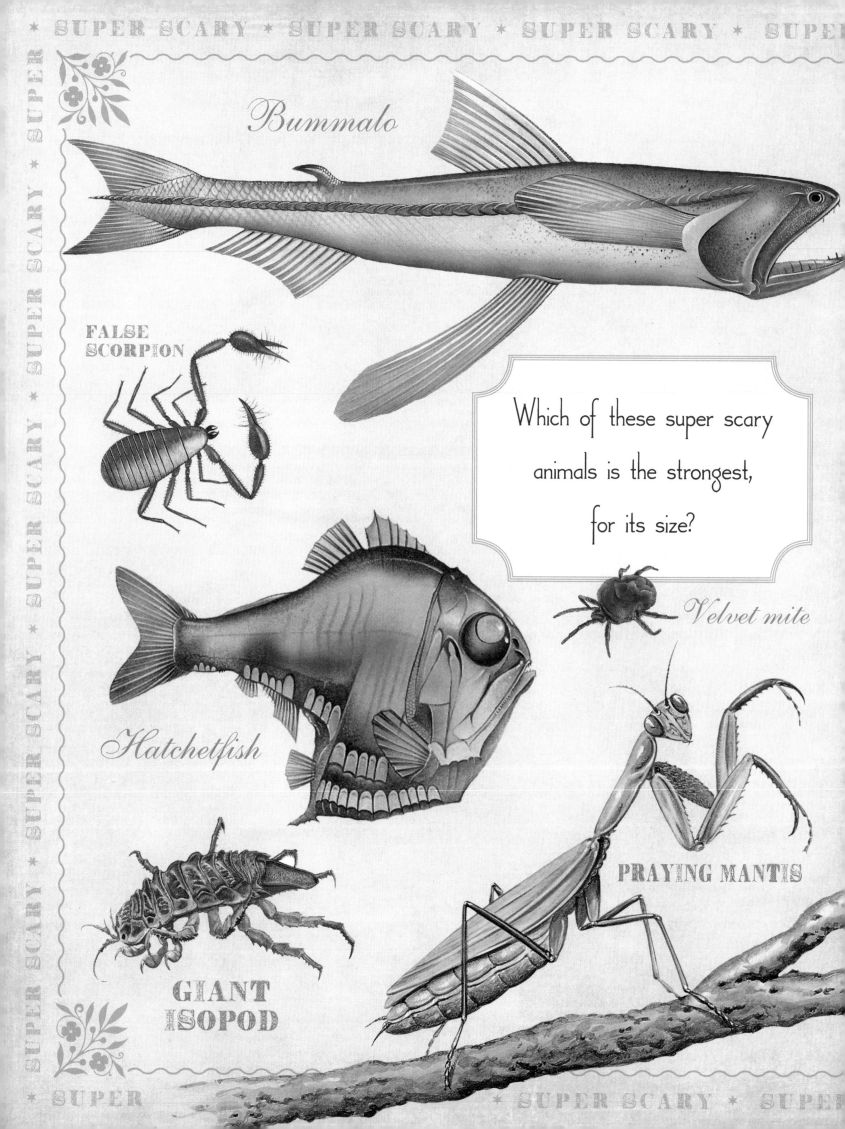

Bummalo

FALSE
SCORPION

Which of these super scary
animals is the strongest,
for its size?

Velvet mite

Hatchetfish

PRAYING MANTIS

GIANT
ISOPOD

Flea

LIONFISH

Stag beetle grub

Tick

DUSTMITE

Boll weevil

STAG BEETLE

Anglerfish

Purse web spider

30 Ladybirds

40 Tadpoles

50

Butterflies and Moths

FENNEC FOX

Koala

Deer mouse

GREAT JERBOA

Long-eared owl

The animal with the smallest ears has probably got the best hearing of them all. Which one is it?

Luna moth

Elephant shrew

RABBIT

GHOST BAT

Springhare

RACCOON

Lappet-faced vulture

African hunting dog

AARDVARK

SLUG

CHEETAH

GIBBON

Garden snail

Jungle runner

Midge

HOUSEFLY

WEDDELL SEAL

Wood turtle

Bottlenose dolphin

CATERPILLAR

Grasshopper

RED KNEED TARANTULA

Three-toed sloth

Roadrunner

Hedgehog

PIRANHA

Flea

If the slug and the snail had a race who do you think would win?

GREATER RHEA

Earwig

RED DEER

Elephant

Stag beetle

PORCUPINE

Marlin

Brittle star

RHINOCEROS

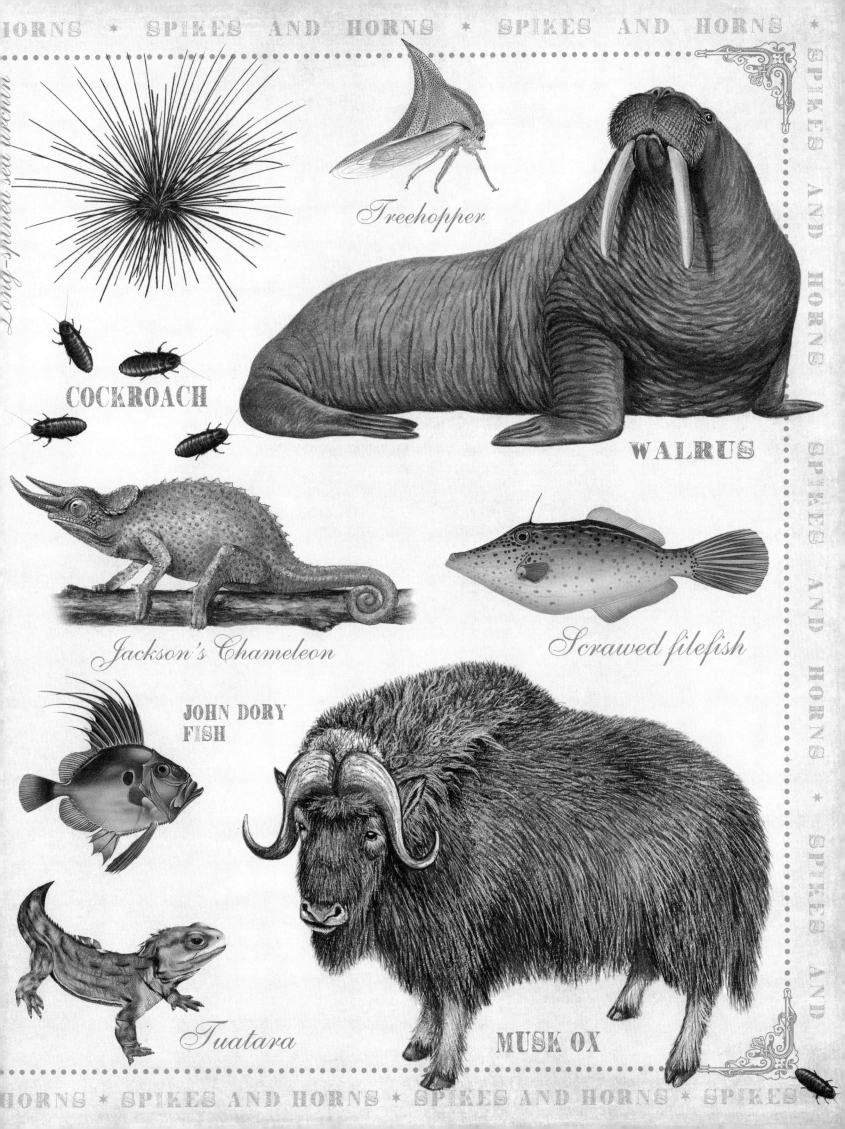

Long-spined sea urchin

Treehopper

COCKROACH

WALRUS

Jackson's Chameleon

Scrawed filefish

JOHN DORY FISH

Tuatara

MUSK OX

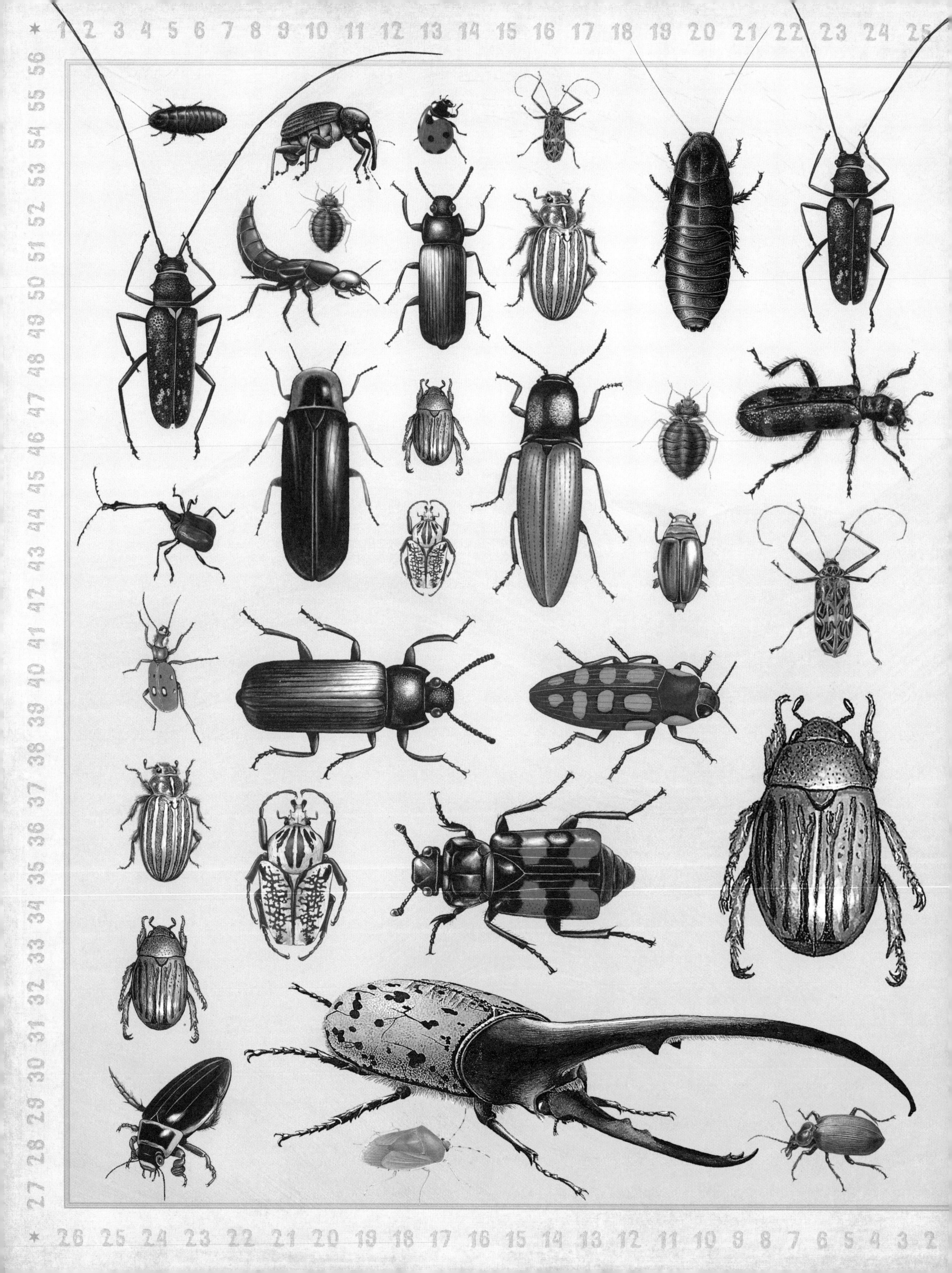
★ 1 2 3 4 5 6 7 8 9 10 11 12 13 14 15 16 17 18 19 20 21 22 23 24 25
56 55 54 53 52 51 50 49 48 47 46 45 44 43 42 41 40 39 38 37 36 35 34 33 32 31 30 29 28 27
★ 26 25 24 23 22 21 20 19 18 17 16 15 14 13 12 11 10 9 8 7 6 5 4 3 2

60
Beetles and Bugs!

BLUE BIRD
OF PARADISE

RUBY THROATED
HUMMINGBIRD

Ribbon-tailed astralia

*King of
saxony bird*

SUPERB
LYREBIRD

*Red-tufted
malachite
sunbird*

Crimson
topaz

RAGGIANAS

Greater bird
of paradise

MARVELLOUS
SPATWETAIL

Quetzal

Royal
flycatcher

WIRE TAILED
MANAKIN

Jewel beetle

Blowfly

SATIN
BOWERBIRD

BLUEFIN TUNA

Blue

Dragonfly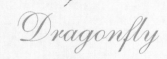

Morpho butterfly

SPOTTED SALAMANDER

BLUE JAY

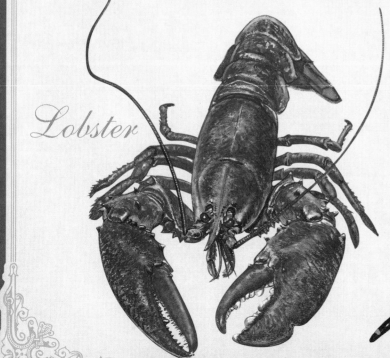

Lobster

FIRE
SALAMANDER

Jellyfish

PURPLE HONEYCREEPER

Purple

Portugese man of war

PUFFERFISH

Whip scorpion

Caecilian

MUDPUPPY

FLOWER MANTIS

Kiwi

EIDER DUCK

TOUCAN

Flamingo

Rainbow lorikeet

TURKEY

PUFFIN

Sparrow

AVOCET

COCKERAL

Goshawk

Hummingbird

Brown pelican

OYSTER CATCHER

Hornbill

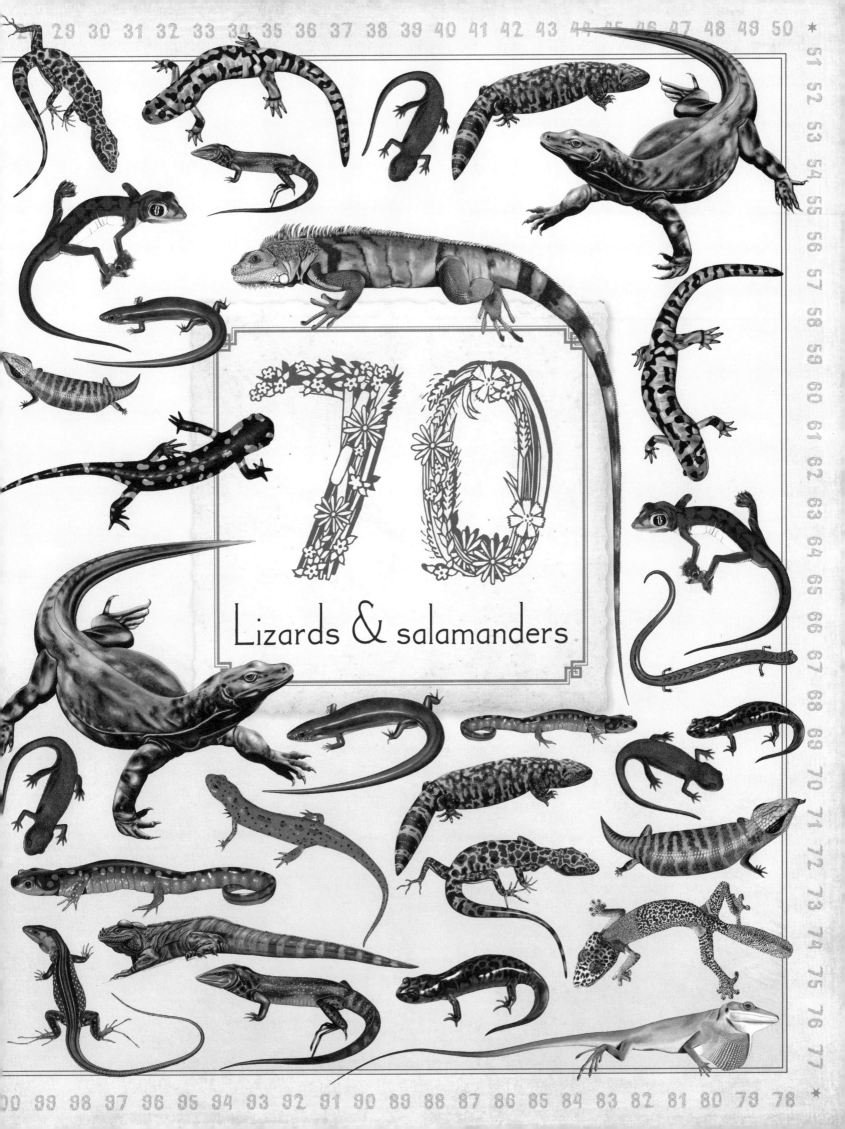

70

Lizards & salamanders

Ant

Wren

CATERPILLAR

OSTRICH

Shrimp

GIRAFFE

Minnows

Bedbug

Hummingbird

ELEPHANT

HIPPOPOTAMUS

Mouse

Silverfish

WHALE

Golden lion tamarin

GOLD FROG

Desert kangaroo rat

Silverfish

Gold

FALSE SCORPION

Golden mouse

IMPALA

LIONS

Hamster

X-ray fish

HARDYHEAD SILVERSIDE

BLUEFIN TUNA

Smelt

Silver

Goldfish

Rough-head grenadier

WILD BOAR

Elephant shrew

INDIAN
ELEPHANT

Paddlefish

Streaked tenrec

MANATEE

ECHIDNA

PROBOSCIS
MONKEY

Gavial
crocodile

Tapir

Who can use its nose to
carry water, pick things up
and stroke its baby?

GANGES DOLPHIN

Giant anteater

Darwin's frog

80

Penguins

Blue-black spider wasp

JACKASS PENGUIN

Woodchuck

Northern jacana

HARP SEAL

Stick insect

GALAPAGOS GIANT TORTOISE

Do the animals with many legs move faster than those with just two?

Funnel-web spider

GREAT JERBOA

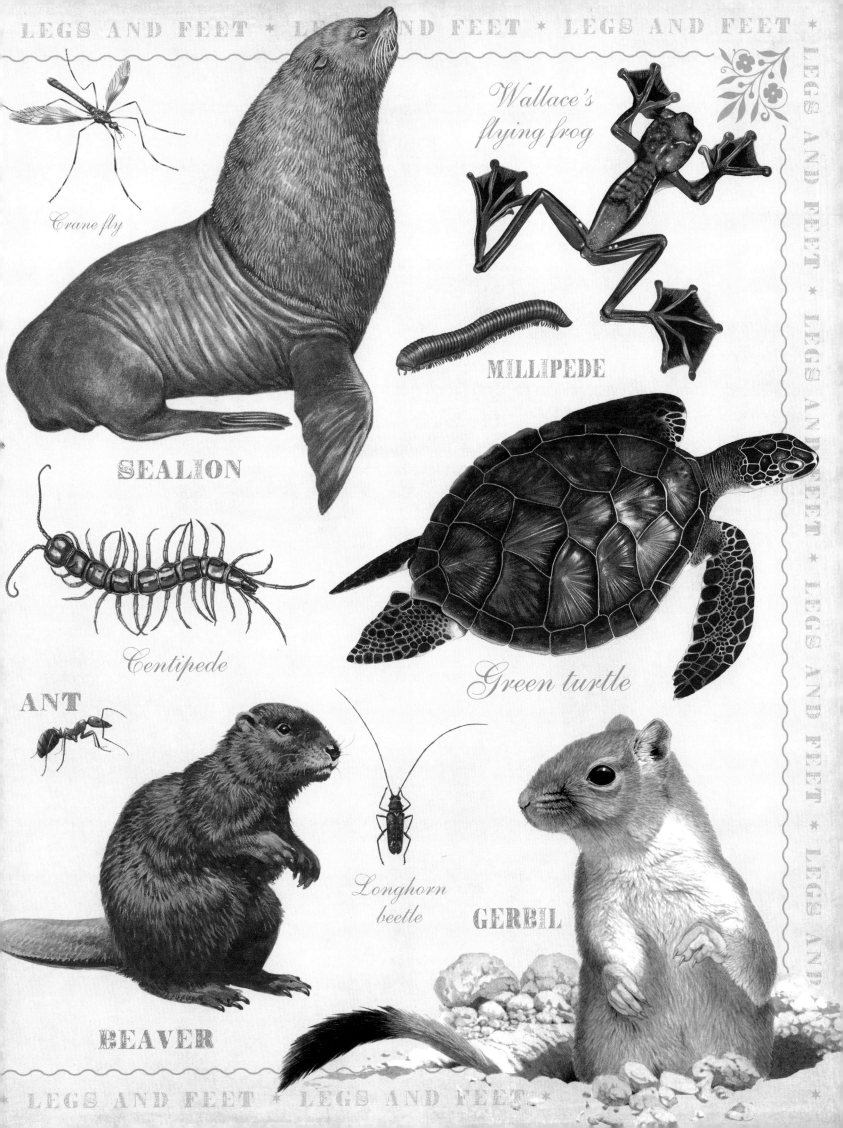

Crane fly

Wallace's flying frog

MILLIPEDE

SEALION

Centipede

ANT

Green turtle

Longhorn beetle

GERBIL

BEAVER

Black widow spider

GREATER SIREN
SALAMANDER

Rove beetle

Black

PANDA

Atlantic manta

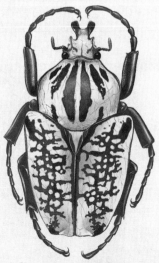

Goliath beetle

GORILLA

POLAR BEAR

ARABIAN ORYX

Arctic hare

White whale

MUTE SWAN

White

Great Egret

Great black slug

CLAM

ARCTIC FOX

90

Flies

Velvet ant

Oleander
sphinx moth

FOOTBALL
FISH

SEA LILY

SOUTH AFRICAN
RAIN FROG

CHAMELEON

Sea anemone

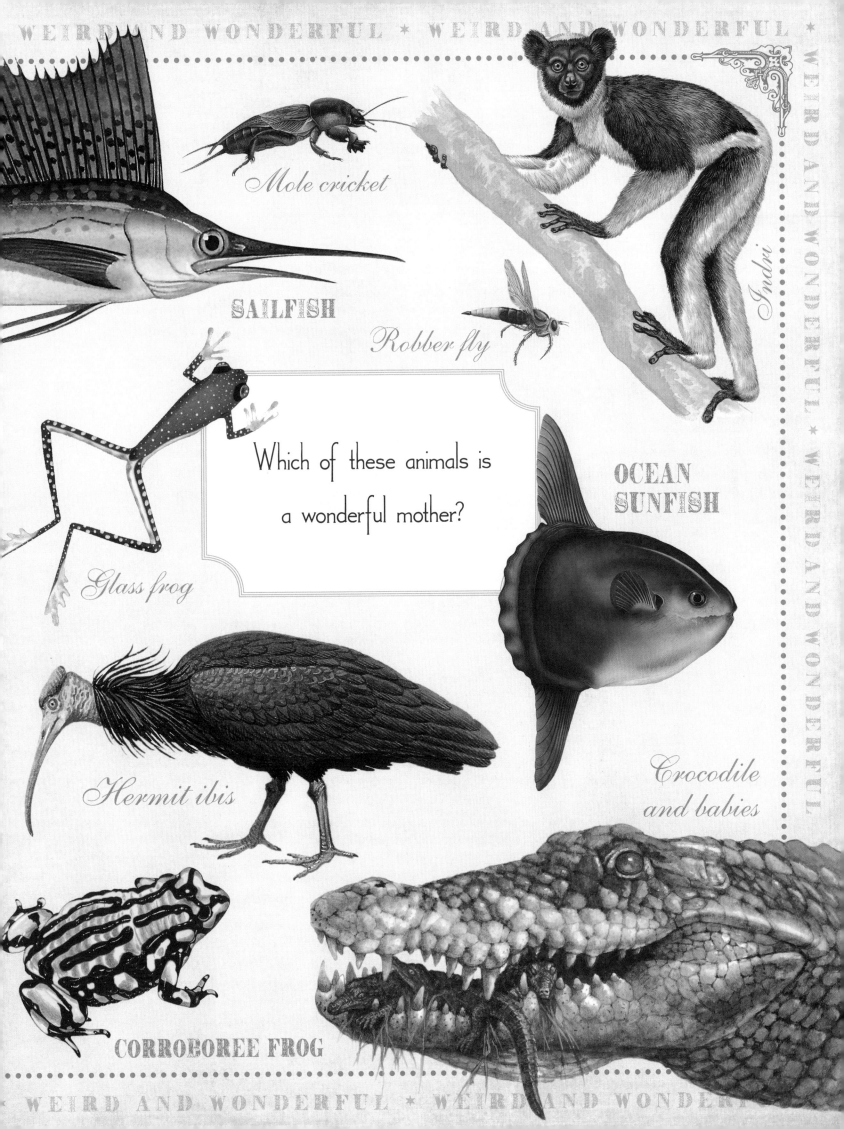

Mole cricket

Indri

SAILFISH

Robber fly

Glass frog

Which of these animals is a wonderful mother?

OCEAN SUNFISH

Hermit ibis

Crocodile and babies

CORROBOREE FROG

Sun
bittern

GREATER GLIDER

EARWIG

Common tern

Long-eared bat

MIDGE

Warbler

OSTRICH

Storm petrel

FLYING FISH

HUMMINGBIRD MOTH

Great black-backed gull

Queen Alexandra's birdwing

Who appears to fly, but doesn't have wings?

Antlion

RED KITE

King vulture

STINGRAY

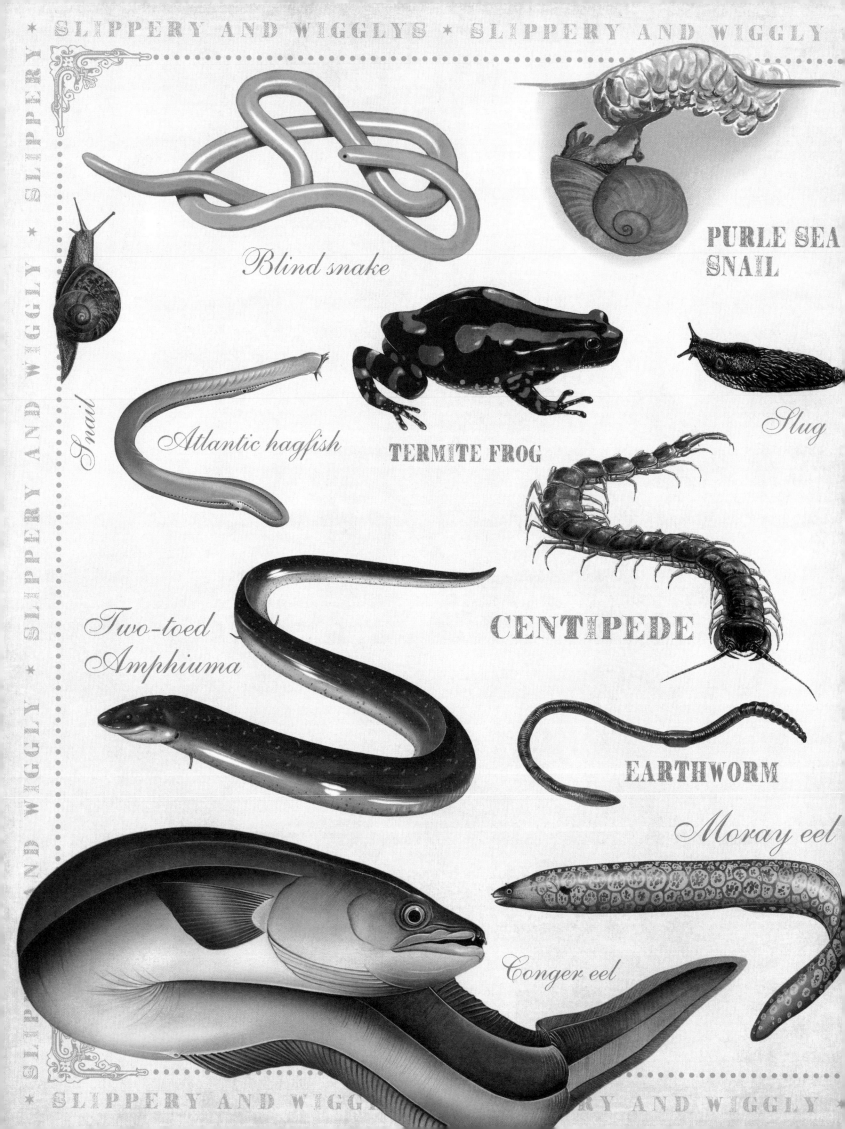

Blind snake

PURLE SEA SNAIL

Snail

Atlantic hagfish

TERMITE FROG

Slug

Two-toed Amphiuma

CENTIPEDE

EARTHWORM

Moray eel

Conger eel

Transvaal snake lizard

OCTOPUS

Nudibranch

SPOTTED WATER SNAKE

Lamprey

CAECILIAN

PACIFIC GIANT SALAMANDER

Ross seal

Paddleworm

1 2 3 4 5 6 7 8 9 10 11 12 13 14 15 16 17 18 19 20 21 22 23 24 25
56 55 54 53 52 51 50 49 48 47 46 45 44 43 42 41 40 39 38 37 36 35 34 33 32 31 30 29 28 27
26 25 24 23 22 21 20 19 18 17 16 15 14 13 12 11 10 9 8 7 6 5 4 3 2

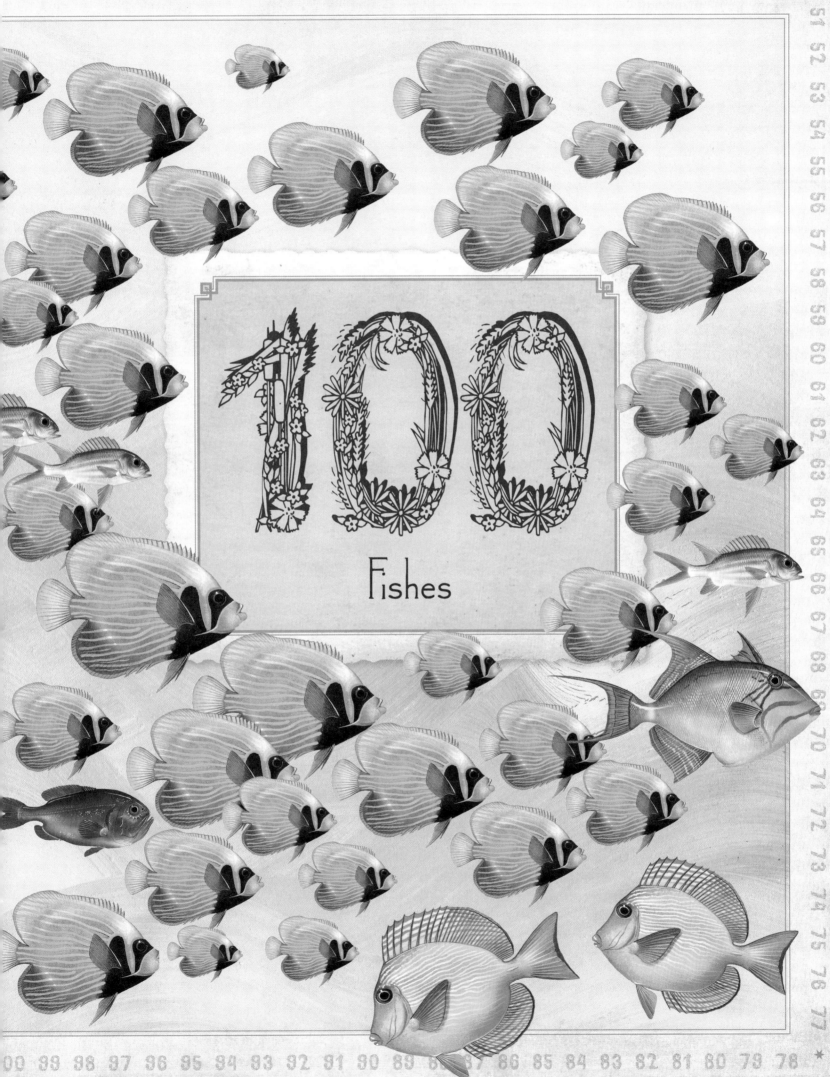

100

Fishes

Red-tailed tropic bird

Emperor tamarin

OLM

CAPE LOPEZ LYRETAIL

KOWARI

Guppy

Which of these creatures has a sting in its tail?

Scorpion

ZORILLA

WEEDY
SEADRAGON

*Meller's
chameleon*

CLUBTAIL
DRAGONFLY

Mayfly

Lumholtz's tree kangaroo

RED
SQUIRREL

Macaw

Desert kangaroo rat

TREE
PANGOLIN

Stonefish

LUMPSUCKER

STURGEON

*Arabian toad-
headed agama*

GIANT
TOAD

Pinecone fish

GIANT
ARMADILLO

Fiddler crab

WARTY NEWT

Sand dollar

Alligator snapping turtle

ARMADILLO LIZARD

Sea cucumber

Dwarf seahorse

SALTWATER CROCODILE

GHOST BAT

Goose barnacle

Scallop

Funnel-web spider

Only mammals have real hair – which animals are faking it?

Firebrat

Surubim

MANED WOLF

AARDWOLF

Porcupine fish

White-lined sphinx moth

ARMY ANT

JAPANESE MACAQUE

CARPENTER BEE

Sumatran rhino

Sun bear

Sea mouse

Wind scorpion

PENGUINS

Arctic hare

Crabeater Seal

Snowy sheathbill

NORWAY LEMMING

POLAR
BEAR

MOOSE

Gerboa

GREEN IGUANA

Secretary bird

Meerkat

INDIAN PYTHON

FIREBUG

Desert night lizard

CAMEL

INTERESTING EYES

Most animals have two eyes - this wolf spider has eight.

Stag beetle

SUPER SCARY

The stag beetle is incredibly strong and for its size, one of the world's strongest beasts.

Wolf spider

Luna moth

Slug

Snail

WEIRD EARS

The moth has very simple ears and can hear better than almost any other animal!

FAST AND SLOW

If these two creatures had a race it would be a very slow one - who knows which one would win?

Indian elephant

Centipede

AMAZING NOSES

The elephant's nose is called a trunk, it is really strong and very useful.

LEGS AND FEET

Four legs are faster than two, but for it's size, the spider, ant and centipede can move very fast with more!

Spider

Scorpion

Ant

Greater glider

TREMENDOUS TAILS

The scorpion protects itself from predators by using its tail to sting.

Crocodile

FABULOUS WINGS

The glider's skin and the fish's pectoral fins help them to glide, but neither have proper wings to fly.

Flying fish

WEIRD AND WONDERFUL

The crocodile is a wonderful mother, she carries her young in her mouth.

Ghost bat

INCREDIBLY HAIRY

These are the mammals with real hair the rest are faking it.

Aardwolf   *Maned wolf*   *Japanese macaque*   *Sun bear*   *Sumatran rhino*